Praise for F

Flight, Kimberly L. Becker's m
sing and images that soar. We ... ges of
the natural world, and narrativ ... voice and Lyme disease,
Becker creates a stunning tapestry of the human experience. All flight is a balance between two sets of forces, lift and weight. In Becker's poems, the lift is the resilience of the human spirit and our desire to fly, and the weight, all that we carry that weighs us down. In her poem "Morning Song," Becker writes:

> All the things you feared, they have come true// still, song
> rises//still, red bud and dogwood// throw forth bloom//
> still, blackbird with red war paint// calls: *iyugwu*

The colloquial translation of the Cherokee word *iyugwu* is "bring it on." This is truly a greeting for each day created by a poet who knows how to rise above all that would hold her down. Savor these rich poems and remember how to listen: to the wisdom of your body, to the stories past and present, to the plants and animals we share space with, and even to listen deeply to the very earth herself.

—Malaika King Albrecht, author of *The Stumble Fields, Lessons in Forgetting,* and *Spill*

What could be more appealing to the poetic imagination of earthbound humans than the act of flying? In this promising and provocative new collection, Kimberly Becker examines every iteration of taking to the air, and the worship of birds, raven, dove, heron, hawk and ibis, and their many habits. War dances make room for somber meditations, and uplifting well-made sentences glide across each page. Freshly squeezed myths and fables populate these narratives and light down in new and unexpected ways, scattering any preconceived notions or baggage that the reader may bring to the table. There are many moments of quiet astonishment, and the wind from the wings of this book stays with you, long after it has settled back in its nest on your shelf.

—Keith Flynn, founder of the *Asheville Poetry Review* and author of *Colony Collapse Disorder*

Flight

Flight

Kimberly L. Becker

MadHat Press
Cheshire, Massachusetts

MadHat Press
PO Box 422, Cheshire MA 01225

The Library of Congress has assigned
this edition a Control Number of
2021930693

ISBN 978-1-941196-73-1 (paperback)

Cover design by Marc Vincenz
Cover image: *Blue Jay* by Joshua Durant
joshuadurantart.weebly.com
Book design by MadHat Press

www.MadHat-Press.com

Other works by Kimberly L. Becker

Words Facing East (WordTech Editions)

The Dividings (WordTech Editions)

The Bed Book (Spuyten Duyvil)

For my warrior son, Alex,
and in memory of our beloved Anna

There must be those among whom we can sit down and weep and still be counted as warriors.
—Adrienne Rich

Table of Contents

REMEMBER

RELEASE

Nvg

REMEMBER

Sogwo

Welcome Dance / War Dance

Leader sends up chilling cry   Other warriors answer
Paint and feather, claw and club   eyes on every dancer

Offer of peace, show of strength   Better our friend than foe
Movements mimic close combat   Blanket spread for orphan, widow

Triptych: Creation, Dove, Raven

I. Creation

It was, as they say, heaven—
the thrust of our wings
molding what humans call valleys
that muscled upward pull
making mountains
          We flew and angled
and sometimes we coasted
The wind in our feathers
(whose breath, the Creator?)
was cold but bracing
and made us feel as one

The strength required to exert against inert earth
was a pleasure of accomplishment
as the mountains rose up in gratitude
and the valleys moaned in ecstasy
No one tells you this but here
we were, agent and witness
          And when we had done this
we circled above in admiration
and spied the river ribboning
and we laughed with joy

Then we played, tumbling and
catching ourselves in the blue

People had not yet been made
And they would emerge from a place
those Real People, *AniYvwiya*

and some towns would be white
and some towns red
and our carrion kin would feed
but that would be later
even though we felt it
and swept away the vision with our wings

And we saw some of our fathers' feathers
array the heads of warriors
But that all came later
First there was just the bustle of creation, the flush
of pleasure in the making
Our eyes saw our completed task
and it was good
It was very good

II. Dove

That damn raven, telling stories: whom do you trust?
It's true I get the credit; when *Corvus corax* went out too

We flew together for a time, but he showed off by flying
faster and kept on, whereas I came back when waters
were still high and cooed the hull to sleep with my lullaby

The man sent me out later (Raven doesn't
take direction well) and by then the waters
had subsided and I found an olive tree
beginning to shoot out its new growth so
I brought that back as proof but what actually
happened was I found Raven sitting in
a cedar tree and joining him asked
where he had been and he told of bodies
floating and I had to ask (curiosity
overcame me) if he had fed on them
and I'll never forget the look he gave me:
such cold disdain: *No of course not*
that's disgusting, but then smiled and I saw red
in his mouth (or was it his lying tongue?)
and with a sharp talon he swiftly plucked something
from his beak that resembled flesh and sniggered

Then he said he had something for me
and produced a branch of cedar:
Take this back to your master why don't you
I thanked him, but told him I would find my own evidence
He shrugged his great black shoulders: *Suit yourself*

then he began whistling, raising his wings in a concerted rhythm
Soon he was singing then scatting like a huckster
I felt he was mocking me when he threw in a coo
then fell into some kind of trance
with his eyes open but somehow unseeing or seeing past
repeating: *kolanv, kolanv, kolanv*
(which I later learned meant *Raven* in his tongue)

He had made a wide nest with sticks and mud and fur
(I thought I glimpsed the gleam of bones)
I started to feel afraid since he was so much larger
Well get along then, he dismissed me
with an outstretched wing in an anti-blessing:
Don't look so surprised and scandalized
The meek shall inherit the earth huzzah

His laughter plagued me as I flew and I was sure
he threw his voice to fool me, but then he would appear
beside me, then below and above, twisting
and cavorting on currents, even coasting
upside down beneath so we became a parallel
flight of the darkest black and brightest white

Suddenly he opened his mouth and screamed with all that red

I almost fainted and plummeted from the sky
but he rolled away into bank of clouds and was gone

I heard his laughter echo through the stillness
as I flew as fast as I could until I found an olive tree to rest upon
in the quiet of the green, but kept checking my back

As my breath evened and I looked out across the land
I saw it had dried and cracked into the most intricate patterns
with pockets of damp where fish flopped and worms straggled
amid new growth rising, and only then did I pluck a sprig
from the olive tree and return it to those waiting for me

And the rest, of course, is history, story on story

III. Raven

Here's what they don't tell you: I flew out with Dove
and at first we soared together but I soon outstripped her

She always was more circumspect, whereas I was content
to row against the currents and I just kept going
flying low over gray waters, a color later called steel by humans

Back then we didn't know the destruction that would come

You always hear about the dove and olive branch
but what they don't tell is my part of the story, or the whole of it
They say I didn't come back but that isn't true
(beware the liars)

I came back to an empty ark, its boards caved in like broken ribs
and I alit on high with a branch of cedar in my beak
the medicine tree they would need, green and fragrant
against the black of my beak … but they had dispersed by then
so there was no one to hear my visions: bloated bodies floating
in the swells or lodged and broken limbs against
jutting rocks or protruding trees, whole families and creatures

And some will say my kind fed on them, but I did not
and you can believe me or not—
since we all have to decide what is truth

And the sun was an eye of knowing
almost cruel in its heat, finally drying
everything, blanching femur and humerus

to the most brilliant white
after flesh had slipped away and become nourishment
for the ravening fish and birds of prey

But all that time I prayed, and finally the waters dried up
yet still I sang a harsh song of renewal because someone had to do it
What else could I do?

And as I sang, the insects gathered in contralto chorus
and the worms writhed and were picked off
By then I was exhausted
so I folded my wings over my head
and over eyes that had seen too much
but I continued to hum and slept with one eye open
so I could see what might be coming
because something always is

Tal

Yellow Tape

At dawn, hawks black against blue
not in strict formation but in a low boil
black over bare trees

Waking to thrum and thrash
of blades slashing ribbons of sky
that fall to drape another body

Thrall of one more manhunt

Even now that sound fills you with dread
makes you search for cover
makes you brace for death

The Hawks at Galax

We watched as they began to boil—first three, then four, next seven, until there were upward of twenty or more. We lost count, caught up in the spectacle of spiral. We circled concrete around winter-barren grounds, our mouths stale with coffee and exhaustion.

Wings tilt in pale sun
This November sky remains
an unread letter

Tomorrow will bring rain (that you will call cleansing) but today: sun. Together, in silence, we watch hawks wheeling until you ask what the Cherokee word for *hawk* is. I can't remember if I ever knew. I say I will find out.

Feathers you gathered
in summer as a child, held
fast in heart-sized fist

Framed photograph of you as a boy, crouched on bigger boulder. You clutch hawk feathers, russet and black, patterned for keeping, while other small hand shields your eyes in unintentional salute. Now you are a warrior.

Dizzying display
of circles counterclockwise
but never release

Ceremony for my father: circling to remember then reversing to let go. Smoke of fire and wash of water. Later you collage your images while I write grief. We both survive from what we salvage.

Spent snow on mountain
December's cold brings fewer
hawks Some still gather

It is counter to my instinct to release, but I can't protect you anymore. We circle sidewalks, cigarette smoke rising. Not sacred, but another form to round the edges of our pain. Hawks boil in my mind. Their wings brush the inside of my brain. It is so hard to stay grounded. Easier to keep watching from above.

Hawks inscribe circles
of invisible contrails
We try to ascend

Years spent circling the same patterns. Naming all the griefs so they can be released, rising like smoke from ceremonial fire. I write *Tawodi* in syllabary and teach you how to say it.

Cedar remains green
not undone by winter's cold
A medicine tree

While we weren't watching, the hawks moved on. Just for today we will act stronger than we feel. You have so much to give. *Don't be like me* I pray. Aloud I say *I cannot lose you.*

Copper

for Billy

My hospice patient tells me that my hair, in the light, is the same color as his dead partner's.

Billy says his partner wore a ponytail as I often do, but today my hair is loose and something about the glint of it causes his eyes to light up and he pronounces, *Copper. Not brown, but copper* I sit in silent deference and feel anointed by his intimacy of shared memory. Billy tells me that after his partner died, he honored his partner's wish that a lock of hair be given to the mother, even though she condemned their love as sin and AIDS as punishment.

His face goes private for a moment. He closes his eyes and touches his graying, curling hair. He is letting it grow long, even though his home health aide says it will add time to Billy's bath. I make a note in my chart that this is spiritually significant. I tell him he is handsome.

We sit in thought for our respective long-haired lovers, past and present. When we return from reverie we talk about religion, all the shit that's in the Bible, who slept with whom or even murdered someone, and remember the old story about Samson and his hair, his strength. We laugh and I hold his hand and he says he's glad I came.

I'll cry later in the car, but I also will remember *Copper* and recall how at a back-to-school-night my son's chemistry teacher showed us how copper burned with a green surprising flame. He gave the reason for it—something to do with oxidation. All I know is I was mesmerized by the transformation and now, having heard Billy say *Copper* for my hair's basic brown, I am reminded that in the light and chemistry of love we see the brightest in each other.

Even a penny, next to worthless, can exhibit a patina, the color of lichen on stone. Turns out lichen is not a single organism but symbiotic partnership. Through that single word *Copper,* my patient has conjured worlds of memory and even though his body is failing in its fight against a stronger lion, his spirit is arrayed and shines with light.

Target Practice

After shooting targets
you finger the delicate pattern
made by impact, raised like Braille
on the back of cardboard

We only share outlines of ourselves

Hope is a devastating thing—
the daring to imagine (you are worthy of)
another ending

Easier to don disguise
remembering how the blind
can read faces with their hands
and confer blessings
on the tricksters

Tso

Recruit

Brek-ek-ek-ex, ko-ax,ko-ax
—Aristophanes, *The Frogs*

Apologies spew from my mouth, an army
of frogs that proliferate and squirm
in sticky mass of abject rue for who I am
I am plagued with shame
I invite humiliation
It is as familiar to me as air
Sorry sorry sorry sorry sorry
I apologize for my very self
Why would you do that? Why would you say that?
I don't know, I whisper, my voice a croak
of pain I cannot name but know so well
I cannot excuse myself; it comes so
easily this place of self-abasement
In the basement of myself is stored self-
abnegation, mess readily accessed
I will apologize for everything
if you will just forgive and love me still
Frogs cling to rocks slick with filamented
moss, place of loss, place where pulses from the past
throb like frogs' distended throat-song
I rasp flaccid excuse in well-versed words
that placate you, diminish me, until
I am the size of those small but loudly
chorused frogs and until those frogs have grown
raucous with raw cries of lamentation
until I am one with that profusion
recruiting all my former sorrow in
service of my new and harsh commander

Interrogation Room

You questioned your body
how it ended up down below
while you watched from the ceiling

He questioned your body
knew the precise techniques
to make you writhe and speak
in convincing lies

Your real secrets were painted
on the walls behind him
blood blown, Lascauxian
straight through hollow bones

You folded up the thunder
laid it docile in your lap
reached and bent the lightning
into arrows for your finely-crafted bow

Hailstones melted down
the gully of your fevered spine

You walked into the flashing ocean
and rode back, a conqueror
on your horse of surf and laid
your trophies on the sand—

conch for calling
coral for cutting

Amnesty Box

No Questions Asked
Not, for example, who last kissed your scar
Nor which lines on your palms stand for life or lies
See? I am a blade, not of weapon, but of grass
that still can cut if handled carelessly
(Scar from cutting with table knife that slipped
still whitecrescents when you bend your trigger finger)
Cram the box full with all our love
(did I say *love?* I meant that to be *live*)
unstable ammunition
Someone else will empty it
and marvel at our unused power
and suffer by our cowardly hand

In Tellico Plains

in memory of Ophah

On the way back
from visiting a dying woman
on her birthday I stop the car

tromp through a field
where memories of mounds are asking
the river for answers

Those places in our lives
where we look for reasons
in our history

Those times in our lives
when we must render our own answers
to the asking river

Nvg

Code Talking

After a while the code lies disused
as our People's language lies under our tongue
rattler ready to spring
Codetalkers, *Diné, Tsalagi*
used words for war maneuvers

No one calls me by the name you gave me
I am not that person anymore / I will always be that person
Choose whichever translates best
Whoever destroys you holds the coded key

Genetics encoded our physical fate
(immune deficiencies
strange fevers of unknown etiology
nightmares that bleed into day with cracked code of truth)

All I can witness to is this:
Your skin on mine made another language
Your lips spoke desire's contorted syllables
I was a child   you taught me to speak
All that's left is this:
too late *I love you, I miss you* in the ICU

The sound of someone coding
We said as much as we could, went as far as we were able
At least we sought the source
One word in native tongue releases years of memories
so better to stay mute

What does it all mean? you asked of all my letters
handwriting cramped and indecipherable

Gray fox fixed me with its gaze
close by maritime forest, paw prints in sand
and the yellow flare of a flower
sent up in emergency

All of it code for something vital
so that when fox cried that night, I woke up and said *I hear you*
Fox   foxtrot
Red heavy receiver linking to commander
These words were always a disappearing act
If she were gone, I could live my life
We turn towards what we think will save us
we turn towards hope and hope it shines on us and leaves us shining

Secret City

in memory of Tammy

They are building the bomb
but it's a secret
They are talking in code
They won't know what they've done until
it's headline news
Now they are united in purpose
They have wooden sidewalks above the mud
Your rollerskates make a thumping sound as you
fly high above the muck
For a child it was safety and sodas
while grown ups worked in secret
arriving on trains not knowing their destination
The prophet foretold it:
the city, the rail road, the engines, people
(thousands), factories, chapel
All hidden by hills tucked behind the river
People who worked in secret on the Gadget
would later whisper: "we built the bomb and didn't know it"
Some things we don't name that are dear
Some things we don't name that are dire
You said to lose me *would be Hiroshima*
This was our secret city, too
Now the hills seem so peaceful
Activists climbed them—
breath and heartbeat and righteousness
Keeping it all in the news
Keeping it all in the light
When shadows were pasted onto sidewalks
The secret was let out
People knew what they had built

And new prophets make headlines so we won't forget
Serving time for sabotage
They know that
~~under the secret lies the secret~~
~~under the secret, the lies, the secret~~
When my patient tells me she wanted to see me so badly
(even though she no longer remembers my name)
I am moved almost to tears
She'd told me all her secrets, too horrific to mention or imagine
Dying, she was finally trying to live past them
She is so skeletal that her port protrudes alienlike
But her vivid blue eyes are bright and I tell her so
She shows me an award won in a nursing home beauty pageant
She asks me to open her window
turns her gaunt face towards the easeful breeze
closes her eyes as morphine kicks in
while white curtains billow in surrender

The Late Unpleasantness

Whether myth or fact, the image is arresting—
wild pigs forage on the dead at Gettysburg
Bloated skin stretches tight with gas and fluid

Along with flesh, the pigs consume letters
meant for loved ones: *My dearest Samantha*
and Bibles gnawed through to that well-worn Psalm:
yea though I walk through the valley of the shadow of death I will fear
no evil—
and yet they did fear, mightily, and alone

All battles vary, but the same sure-snouted devourer wins in the end

You sent us clambering up some statue to slip sunglasses on a general
then captioned the photo: *Who's that behind those Foster Grants?*

Years later I returned to find that the dead still inhabit these hills

Then there's the family rifle got off Union enemy—
my son hoists it to his shoulder
with the ease of someone strolling into battle

Red Ibis

Having just agreed to separate
but with no itinerary for this space between
decision and action, we drive to Baltimore
to the same aquarium we took our son
to when he was young

At the top of the aquarium, damp
in simulated rain forest, we walk
among the outsized, almost fetid plants
as birds fly up and scream at confines of the skylight

Beyond the bay, the ocean pulls
Do birds remember where they come from
or were they born to this captivity?

The red ibis sits quiet among the green
Not bright yet, like the British redcoat
I'll drive hours to see on my own
enamored of its blood-red wool and garish
golden buttons
Catawba girl will make a snide remark
to me as Cherokee—hatred carried forward
like a tattered battle standard
colors faded yet discernible for loyalty

This red ibis isn't a true red
Still young, it is the color of dull rust
like blood dried long ago

We stand in a temporary truce admiring
its plumage, not knowing the worst of our

domestic war is yet to come, that will be
waged in regalia of rage

You walk ahead to look at other displays
but I stay on and watch
what isn't happening

The bird does nothing as far as I can see
yet in its muted beauty I want it to confer
a kind of benediction on the coming devastation

But the bird is unaware of this demand
Just as we are unware of the protracted
engagement that will come to sunder our long alliance
(gold rings exchanged once more, this time for cash)
when even peaceful memories will be stained
and stiff like bandages that have bound the wound
of a long-delayed and brutal amputation
by a field doctor with only chloroform for pain

So that at the end, after the notary
has signed and stamped our story
when you move to embrace me goodbye
I will shut the door on what had been
our family home, now a final stronghold
to protect my son

But we didn't know that at the time
We only saw the bird standing still
as a herald or crest on coat of arms
so that when I recall this time I will see in its form

a grace and calm before we armed ourselves
to fight the last battles of our uncivil union

I will come to think of you, ex-husband
and weep with reddened eyes
for all we failed to have

And the ibis?

May the young bird that we saw that day
far from the Amazon shore
age until its feathers brighten to scarlet hue
while our golden-sealed divorce decree
declares us free to fly—alone

Hisg

Erasure

A year after we never met
I remember something else—
how as a child you'd comb the beach
rescuing crabs or jellyfish
          the injured gull dragging its wing across the sand

When you'd wake at night or early morning,
when street light or sunlight
lay like hand or brand across her face

you'd wonder for a knife's edge of an instant
if my love had been real
even if buried
underground
with all the other warriors
protecting what was left of you

My emperor, I answer: yes

So that you may rest
I guard even your forgetting

Ouroboros

I say: let's go to Nepal and see the Crystal Monastery
You say: the pond here is fine and has two chairs beside it
Next day: earthquake and ruin

I cannot bear the tenderness of touch

We call the clouds to us
They roll in like stealth bombers
We are pleased at our enchantments

It was only a small murder
We did it together
We tried to bury guilt with the body
Crucifix of sticks and plaited grass
The field is soon grown over

When I woke up, it was yesterday
Owl swiveled its head to survey past and future

I slipped sideways into your dream

I find your lighter in my bed
I wear your shirt that holds the scent of you

Phones glow like icons in our hands
Your text says *everything is sacred*
I read it as *everything is scared*
and both seem true

Broken Formula to Bind One's Lover

The night before you saw him
thunder shook the mountains
Morning: river swollen

When you saw, you had to have him
so you conjured his affections
followed close behind
stepping silent, stone to stone

while he fished but never saw you
only shadow, your intentioned tears
falling
in the bright
of the shallows
becoming shimmer fish he caught and ate

In this way you gained entry
ensuring gut reaction
so that when he saw, he hungered for you
to the point of stinging tears
not understanding why when he cried
river gathered him into her long arms

Now at night you hold and murmur
close by your now-bound lover
words designed to keep him as he sleeps
drawing circles with saliva
over thunder of his heart
hoping to harness his rivering blood
to your dark and fastening source

Sacrifice

naked, you begin to grass dance on the carpet

shoulder blades rising in rhythm

later you roll beads to conjure on me

when you shot the bear between its eyes

it took its human form and it was you

you butchered your own body

ate it, hung your neck

with splay of claws

Sudali

Night Drive from Nashville

moon over mountain
that long division
trust divided by betrayal

the moon seems to play
hide and seek
but it is you who move

you flick on the high beams
and pray no deer
will leap in front of your car

dark pines enclose the road
as you grip the steering wheel
more tightly

Collateral Damage

Sliver of glass escaped notice—you stepped on it
and it took straight to flesh
burying too deep for tweezers' reach
For weeks each step inflicted pain

Long past that minor injury, you imagine how an MRI machine
might draw out embedded memories
                    pulling

to the surface all the damage of the years

    [as shrapnel can work its way out over decades
    body purging itself of
                    fragments
    years after initial injury
    in ongoing acts of organic valor]

Bright Star Whose Name I Never Knew

You want to show me something

We go up to your balcony and there's the telescope
you've built: a circus cannon aimed at the moon

You insist I look, and there's the moon's surface like a Styrofoam ball

You describe its night and day and suddenly my eyes fill
with tears at its far and sullen beauty

This is how our intimacy begins—sharing novel things
and mistaking excitement for Eros

The moon is waxing

You show me Saturn and Spica
that bright star whose name I'd never known

You built the telescope for your children
ground the glass then applied the polish
and in that labor created livable luster

The moon enduring assaults is still peering back
in obdurate existence, mirror to our own endurance
in the face of unexpected griefs
ground and buffed until almost bearable

Later, you move in with your Russian girlfriend
taking your telescope with you
but before, I hear you both above—

laughter and wine glasses, stargazing
while the moon is waning

Glass: A Fugue

There is nothing more surreal, nothing more abstract than reality
—Morandi

Oh music swims back to me
—Anne Sexton

For now we see through a glass, darkly; but then face to face
—1 Corinthians

i.

In the antique shop your then-husband pronounced it all junk, but you persisted, finding several old apothecary bottles he prized as subjects for paintings during his Morandi phase. Morandi had painted the same bottles over and over at different times of day. Bottles wavy and dimpled and pitted with age that had held tinctures and bitters, remembering bottle of Mercurochrome your grandfather hastened to apply to every wound and then—mind-elongating thought like blown glass—remembering how Whitman moved among the wounded in Washington. That was after you had bought the bottles and after he had arranged them on the windowsill where the cat would stretch out on the radiator of the centuries-old house with its imperfect and prismatic glass and crystal knobs on every slamming door.

ii.

Driving I-75, peering through rain-spattered windshield, you remember those bottles, their shapes and planes, various stoppers, colors not quite colors, more like tinges and tints of watercolor and wonder at how important it was to you that you discover them for him. Years prior he had first pointed some out in the window of an antique shop and you desperately wanted to buy them for him, but the store was shut. Even now you recall the glint of sun on the storefront window where inside glowed aqua, amber, ruby, and rarest violet, glass. What does it mean that you remember those unbought bottles better than the color of your husband's eyes?

iii.

In Murano the air was wavy with heat. Glass blowers used flame to form their luminous art like the millefiori paperweight you bought for a souvenir. We could no more retrace and unspool our misdeeds than the blowers could unbreathe their molten shapes. In Venice a cold glass of water formed flowers of condensation. Pressing it to your forehead you looked through to your husband's face, wondering what trace of you would remain on the glass.

iv.

In St. Mark's Square Moorish clock kept time for boorish tourists. In 1291, glassblowers were forced to move to the island of Murano for fear of fire in Venice. Shattered glass scattered like hard candy: butterscotch yellow or peppermint-striped (stuck together in clumps like in that heavy crystal dish in your grandparents' house). When you took your turn at blowing glass, the circle formed was out of round and heat made it hard to breathe. After clearing cabinets of liquor bottles, you heaped crash of colors in recycling bin.

v.

How many times did Morandi paint his bottles in a shifting light?

All the bottles ranged along your windowsill—how light shone through them, creating patterns on the hardwood floor that was once your son's room, narrow as a ship's berth.

On a school field trip to replica of a schooner, deck prism drew light beneath the darkened deck.

There you bought a prism you could use as paperweight, but don't. Instead, it sits atop black bookcase, casting aqua light on the wall behind.

vi.

The phlebotomist arranges glass tubes in rows and quickly switches when drawing blood to try to solve the mystery or confirm what was suspected. It is your last act of caring to insist on going with him.

Then in Little Italy the exchange that would be our final break: *Are we doing the right thing?* Then, after long pause as you gripped your coffee mug, *Based on our history, yes.* That was our Horseshoe Bend, but in reverse.

For years your anger remained brittle, ready to shatter. You read about the glass eye of a soldier killed in battle and how someone found and pocketed it as talisman, heavy like a cat's eye marble.
How did we fail to see what was coming?

vii.

The time he used stalk of sea oat to write in Greek on sand at the beach. *It seems to me that everything is good.*

Being pitched towards windshield glass when he would brake in rage.

Now windows are boarded up against a hurricane. Eerie stillness of the eye.

Only then does it come back to you that sand is the key ingredient in glass.

We are formed from what has crushed but not destroyed us.

Galgwoq

Provisions

Every morning you wake up and reassemble
your heart—chamber to valve—until it resembles
a fist, clenching and unclenching ungraspable
rage, because at night—the long undoing—
you bypass all feeling, for to feel
would require confronting the prognosis
hardtack of fact, instead of those rationed
rationalizations knowing he would go to her
and while you lay alone they would be coupling
and there was nowhere for you in it

You can see that, but to write it makes it real
so you can eat the hurt
like a case of unrequited pica
so you would almost rather hibernate
like the bears you saw readying for winter
preparing for that long denial
when hearts are stilled to only what is
necessary

Bears' hearts can slow to just eight beats
a minute, letting them live off
the fat of memory, of summer
fields and autumn's fall of acorns

So too with your imaginings—acorns
fallen from the tree Desire and oaks that
never grew, causing you to move inward
where remembrances are stored for living on
metabolized for sustenance

Once a bear found cake consigned to compost
and tongued frosting's granulated sweetness
until only a few crumbs graced his face

You are those crumbs, that ravaged cake
bees will festoon with their
gold and black insignia of rank

Painted Trillium

I wanted to tell you I found your favorite flower
while out walking in the woods trying to forget you
It was white with an inner wash of red,
peace and wartime hues

I didn't pick, didn't photograph it, just admired
then crushed with warring thoughts its fragile head:
Every time I think of you I still want white
Every time I think of you I still see red

Pocketing the Shells

for Allison

The weight of the shells in my pocket
reminds me of those we collected at the beach

Unloaded guns rattle
like rocks in the back of my car

Never figured you for a gunrunner, you say
The fine family, all of us
We laugh the way survivors do

Tears blur my driving vision
and the car keeps veering over the yellow line
treacherous black ice

Nowhere feels like home except a needle in the vein
Burst of heat followed by vast distances
Someone calling my name and prophesying:

When you burn through illusions like scraps of paper
wisdom still waits at the base of the mountain

A long war to know the self
all the campaigns end up here

pocketing seashells
unloading ammunition, shell by shell

Locking the guns in the safe
(note already written: *dagiyaweg*)

River encased in ice
Spent casings scattered on frozen earth

The shells, black as crow feathers
shaking in your pocket

as we force ourselves to dance

The Raven Mockers

In the rooms of the dying
they hover
eager to take the heart
and leave the body
You pray against this force
and it is exhausting
At the moment of death
there is a great gathering of energy
that some mistake for peace
You have spent too much time with the dying
Your own spirit grows thin and frayed
Your own heart is in danger

Even photographs of bones contaminate
All the defilement of graves:
it is not enough to repatriate
We don't like to gaze at death like white people do

You confronted it once: dark mass, pushing against your back
taller than a human, black as shadows' shadows
Another time a cat on the porch tried to look benign
but you recognized it
Same with that crow who fussed and gazed too long
Violent dreams from which you woke with deep scratches

You let them know you knew their name
You declined to feed their power through fear
You and your elder patient pray in Cherokee
Your mistakes make her laugh

When she finally sleeps, you keep watch as long as you can

RELEASE

Sogwo

Nikwasi Warriors

At Nikwasi
grass was sprayed with herbicide
rendering the mound brown

We walked it anyway, circling
in honor of miniature warriors
who spilled from mound to rout
an onslaught of cavalry

Don't underestimate the smallest mounds
the low-slung hills

Not every indwelling force
is apparent at the peak

Survivor Song

in memory of A. S.

Sometimes when flashbacks overwhelmed
you'd sit and hold your patient's hands
while his great tears fell
from blind and milky eyes
his body wracked in sobs

You prayed what Hebrew prayers you knew
into his barely-hearing ears

Once the young rabbi came
and taking him into his arms
sang the old and healing songs
until his elder cried aloud with joy

Later his repeated cries are only of *hello* and *water*

You will guide the straw to his mouth
tattooed number on his arm blurring
before your tears you try not to let spill
You never tell him you are also
from a holocausted people

You will never forget him

The way he used to say *You're beautiful!*

The way you'd say with laughter *You're blind!*

The way his quick kisses on your hand
marked you indelibly with song

Tending the Dying

Sometimes the dead follow you home
and post themselves in your room at night
at the end of the bed or behind the silk curtains

sentries to your dreams, they chatter
sometimes so loudly that you have to ask
politely, if they wouldn't mind talking more quietly

You start setting out just a little food for them on small plates
so they won't be hungry on their final journey
You will miss them when they cross over

when you are left with only your own blanket of lies
standard issue, rough like steel wool
but warm against the chill of truth

The Woman at the Knoxville Zoo

Oh, bars of my own body, open, open!
—Randall Jarrell

And now in another city I find
myself one lunch hour alone at the zoo
where I stand before the raven's cage
and read the sign that says he speaks and that
his name is Edwin, so I address him
by his name and watch his beak to see if
he will speak to me
I wait and nothing
happens except a mother with a stroller
pushing past as her restrained toddler points
"Bird!" with sticky finger
The mother says
with forced brightness *yes, that is a raven*
They guard the tower of London … London Bridge
is falling down, falling down, falling down
They keep moving and once they are out of
earshot, the raven clears his throat and speaks

—It's usually more important that we listen
People call me stupid when I don't deign
to speak on command. Kids throw rocks. My wing
was broken once

—That's terrible. I'm sorry

—It healed up okay. Just aches in damp and
cold. Like England (laughs) *If ravens ever*
leave the Tower of London, the monarchy
will fall. So the lore goes, but the legend's

rigged—how are we supposed to fly away
when our wings are clipped to ensure we stay?
People called Ravenmasters are the ones
with that grim task; I wonder how they sleep
and what they do with remnants of our wings?
I can't fly far in this place, but sometimes
my spirit travels past the confines of this cage—
I like to feel the rush of wind (closes
eyes and seems to go to some private space)
and (pauses, searching for words to describe)
remember all the old stories as I
fly to the highest tree on the mountain
and look down and see the valley's shadows
and the shadows of clouds on the mountains

I like to dive and turn and fly upside down
to change perspective of my view but you—
you stand in the shadows and think the sun
is never coming back. Whatever cage
you think you're in, your spirit doesn't have to stay
People like to confide in me because
they see my captivity as their freedom
to release their questions, concerns, and dreams
sometimes even their plans for suicide
I am like the ones you call priests in black cassocks
But I think you've come to ask permission
to heal. Odd isn't it? People have no
trouble suffering, embrace it actually
Crying (odd trick I haven't learned) can release
some pain, but so can telling to another
Recount your losses to me. I'll listen

So I speak softly to the raven, who
does not interrupt or commiserate
but who is attentive without being
anxious, caring without patronizing
When I'm finished, I realize I have cried
and Raven reaches through the bars and wipes
my tears with a soothing sweep of feathers
from the wing that had been broken

—You've served your sentence of sorrow long enough
Go and listen to someone else; in that
way we free each other from our prisons

I move away from Raven,
turn and raise my hand in thanks and farewell
seeing my fingers first as if feathers
my arms as if they just might become wings

Tal

Illumination

in memory of J.R.L.

My son's whistling sounds like yours
and brings you back to these same roads

where you rigged telephone wires
and labored in green overalls

I remember the tale you told
of how you gave light to the county

I still have that electrical counter you handed me as a child
I'd play with it in the car and click through miles

I still return to it sometimes, watching the numbers
tumble over like the roll of generations

Layover

The cedars of Seattle are dark green against the gray

Now is the time to decide what you want
Don't dissolve like powder in the drink of someone else's life

I meet a bridge builder on the flight
Bridges must be built to flex or they'll collapse
They're vulnerable to attack

That bridge in Charleston half-collapsed, half hung above the water
A new bridge was built alongside the ruins
but it was the broken bridge that scared you as a child

Some things can only go so far

In Alaska there are no bridges on your journey
just ice roads and bush planes

In Seattle you wait hours for someone who never does arrive

Orders

At your funeral in Arlington
I told myself I wouldn't cry
and I didn't:

not when they folded the flag
not when they presented the flag to your widow
not when they fired the salute

not til afterward
on the way home
remembering your long illness

remembering your room at the residential hospice
that looked out into hills and trees
and how you always liked the curtains open
so you could see what was out there
so you could assess for threat

remembering how
when your sight failed
you listened keenly
and how
when your voice failed
then strength failed
you still gave orders
with squeeze of hand
that we all hastened to obey

Viole(n)t

for Robert

Finally you return to painting
Mostly miniatures
You favor purple and florals
where I would have expected
abstract gash of reds

Violet is the darkest true
spectral color
at the edge of vision
rare and ancient in its use
connoting royalty and valor

You haven't cried since Vietnam
You are still that medic
who could not save a friend
But you control this field of canvas

Tso

Death Rattle

Until finally you don't fear death anymore

It's not such a long journey after all

Your breath rattles as you smile or try to

You keep an eye on lead dancer's rattle held high

You fall in place and follow

and find you never were alone

Color Wheel

Sometimes you still spirit-walk
through my dreams
that circle until daytime

You come to me again
in paint of red and black
trick of memoried light

while rainbow delves
beneath the earth
wheel of color, loop of life and death

Bound

in honor of Nancy Ward and other women warriors

We fought always, sometimes
binding our breasts so other soldiers
couldn't guess our sex—after running
we would rest, try to catch our breath
pleurisy stabbing as if knife to ribs
Bound, our breasts reminded us of the stress
of weaning children, of breastfeeding,
cries causing our milk to let down, leaking
through bandages we'd used to lash them tight

Eventually our once coveted supply
would dry and return our breasts to normal
though changed from younger days when cold hands
of our first nervous lovers kneaded them
too hard and clumsily, whereas later
our husbands would tip one into his mouth
as if sipping from a chalice while his fingers
worked the other nipple, igniting more desire

Often it was in the losing of love, where we
felt the most enflamed with expended effort
These odd and fleeting thoughts would arrive
as we scattered across fields already bloodied
with bodies, our breasts secure under the fabric
that ungendered us. Fear engendered courage
much like in childbirth, striving towards an outcome—

Ravaged bodies, chests torn apart
made us think of other battles, sisters
who lost breasts to disease, flesh eaten away

in some cases to the bare-bird rib cage
We are bound to all: women   men   children

We are bound to our people so we fight
some with bound breasts and shorn hair under caps
some with breasts heavy under quickened breath
and flying tangled lengths of straight black hair
some of us taking our dead husband's place
taking up his gun, his cause,
and with a mother's vengeance rallied on
to try to save other mothers' children
for our tribe, for those who would come after us

Hand over heart hand over breast we pledge
bound as we are to the blood of our kin
to fight until our last foe is vanquished

Going to Water

for Paula

Warriors apply paint
black and red for death and life
prepared for either

Fires burn at distances
red towns and white towns
war towns and peace towns

A warrior woman goes to water
At the river she remembers her People
When the first cry goes up her blood answers, her prayer counters

Nvg

Suddenly, the Heron

We walk along the river
A squirrel fusses in a pine

Ice faces stare from the rocks
The trail is muddy with melt

Suddenly a heron, blue expanse, flies
low over water, doubled by reflected image

We stop in our tracks
How not acknowledge this gift?

We go as far as the bridge
the water below ice cold

then turn back on that same path
where laurel speaks in tones of green

Suddenly, the heron
surprises us by flying back

Same astonishment of blue arrival
Again we stop and hold our breath

Was it the same heron?
Are we our same selves

coming and going,
along the same yet changing river?

Ceremony in Lieu of a Funeral

in memory of my father

Lies to soothe the dying:
I forgive you
It doesn't matter
I love you, too

You keep picking through the alphabet for words to say goodbye
for words to bless the ICU and oxygen tube

The way his mouth opened like a bird when you moistened it with
swabs
the softness of hands you'd never held except as a child

Prayers ascend with smoke

Circling this way you remember
circling that way you release

Water's current carries what you can't

Morning Song

Birds wake and throw their songs against the world
I rise and add my own morning song
nogwo sunale nigalsda

Yet I don't feel like singing
my voice is choked with tears
gvyalielitse Yihowa

Somewhere a bear is waking up
like the one whose prints I witnessed in snow
My dog pushed her nose into those impressions
that looked so human

My son carved a soapstone *yona* for me
I keep it safe with shards from Jerusalem
and Manassah gifted by a friend

All those things you feared, they have come true
Still, song rises

Still, redbud and dogwood bloom
while blackbird with red war paint
calls: *iyugwu*

Questing

for all the warriors

Awi Usdi

People neither hear nor heed
my warning so there are consequences
I may be Chief, but I still
need warriors and barring
that
must strategize
So we conceived of vectors,
tick being easiest,
small in size yet so toxic to the victim
after furtive attachment
We employed
this armored middleman
to send our warning message
about needful balance

Prologue

What was the tick telling you?

Bite and bullseye, spreading red

Two days since the bite
& you see white—
Awi Usdi at road's edge:
You haven't asked permission
There is a right and balanced path:
duyukta

Turtle beak once mute reconstitutes
in song of shaking shells bound to women's legs
With men they keep the balance
in the rhythms of the dance
But when rhythms are displaced
tradition disgraced, and earth
does not absorb our offered song
there is a break at source

And still the redbud throws forth its blossom
And still the red-winged blackbird with her slash of war paint
issues a cry of challenge:
are you enemy or ally? declare yourself or prepare to fight

All the things you feared came true
How to go on in your grief?
Luminous eyes of cattle before slaughter: orbs hold worlds

Genetics twisted into swastikas we eat—
Give us back our medicine
Where are all the warriors?

Awi Usdi

I warned them: ask permission
before you kill my brother
I warned them what would happen
but they failed to listen, so
now there are consequences
Blood has been spilled without prayer

without honor, without shame
I warned you, but you chose not
to pay attention
Now you suffer the result
as I send sickness on you

Tick

In a questing pose, front legs outstretched
    I reached out, waiting for your warmth to pass
(O, sweet blood of human animal!)
    Little Deer carried me himself
with strict instruction to attack
    only the two-legged creatures
this time to get your attention
    But first he let me feed on him
giving his own blood sacrifice
    for he only is immortal
whereas I have just a few years
    Humans think they have forever
so you needed a clear message:
    hard to misread a red bullseye
Isn't that what some call sin? Greek:
    hamartia, missing the mark
Rash decisions with no reason
    so I attach and crawl to soft
defenseless flesh—numb you so
    you won't notice my toxic
bite for which you seek cures, but pain
    and weakness will persist

You are not immune [to] this time
As *Ixodes scapularis*
my hard body is as armor
the fate of your world dependent on mine

Plants

Deer ticks cling and quest, waiting, poised
Opportunists alert for hosts to pass
We always tried to help by taking your part
Even when the animals at Council
turned against you, even when some of you
left the human race to become bear clan
even then we continued to help you
Here, make of this a poultice, warm compress
to hold to red and help to draw the poison from your system
On our own we have a hard time getting
your attention since we are not vocal
in the same way as the animals
And although we do speak, you have not practiced
listening for our voice so you take us for granted
as we quietly offer up our medicine
Recognize us as healers; gather up
what will help you most, thanking us as you do so
You have failed to use what is available
and negligence can be as bad
as outright exploitation—our roots grasp
firm as we reach, questing, for the light
We also provide shade so you can rest
but rest should come in balance to your work

and you have not worked at protecting us
even though some of us are also warriors:
tobacco and cedar for starters
We watch and remember all of this
Over years and generations elders
tried to teach the younger but they didn't listen
Who is left to tell the sacred stories?

Blood

At the first sign of attack
we mount defense on your behalf
working to free your hostage heart

As cells multiply and change properties
we circulate petitions for release
We alone remember and so set up sentinels
to watch for known adversaries
as well as new intruders
(You mixed bloods often go to war against yourselves)

We, too, are mostly water
Memories circulate in us from generations back, some secrets
        revealed in vials
of sluggish sediment
Other secrets lie dormant

We will fight until death
even when weak and depleted
even when you refuse to be transfused

Yet sometimes we are forced to forfeit fight
becoming septic while your organs start to fail

Still, as women's issue our power
can benefit the People

Our pressure urges your respect for the blood of other creatures, even
opportunistic tick
that gorges on our source from oblivious hosts

We balloon tick's body until it is yanked from skin and smashed,
disgorging red
We are the color of warriors' paint
We are the red that sustains or stills a life

Human

I gathered flowers for a dying woman's birthday
not knowing tick was questing
When I found it, embedded, it resisted
removal from host of my body
feast of my blood   Later: fever, spreading red
Even now, fatigue and pain can overwhelm me
That's when I think of Little Deer and what
the tick was telling me: P*ay attention—*
don't ignore the world and your connection
to all that dwells therein
You are just part
Some of you are born more sensitive
Even so, you sometimes ignore signs until

illness befalls you, reminding you
of the great imperative in life:
Be the person who listens and not just listens,
but who tells what you have heard
Then act!

Water

Little Deer still comes to water
Sometimes for ceremony, sometimes to swim
antlers poised above the surface like driftwood
Sometimes he stands still and drinks
but never falls in love with his reflection
knowing how narcissism distorts truth
and how we must look past ourselves
He always thanks me for my gift
of coolness and of cleansing power
Sometimes he comes with others
guarding the females and fawns
Sometimes he comes near the large deer
the elk, and when one was hit by car
and its leg was badly broken,
he set and doctored it himself
and helped her to the Magic Lake
Some people come to water and it pleases me
so much that tears of joy flow
with their carried prayers
The ones who sacrifice,
not just for themselves, but all
are the ones who listen best

If more people came to me
there would be more balance in the world
And the plants that crowd my banks stand ready to help treat
not just bodies but spirits wasted by grief of centuries—
blood memories, inflamed pain that never healed because never
acknowledged
I can cleanse it if you let me
but pain is like any person: it wants to be recognized
before healing can begin
and most people turn not to what would help
but to what would numb—
(as tick numbs before it bites)
If they don't feel their own pain how can they possibly feel
—and if feel, then respond—to pain within the world?
So I keep moving and washing away what I can
Some waters stand still to heal, some hidden lakes
and those too are a blessing
And then there are the larger waters:
oceans whose waves of abrasive salt can heal
the wound even as it stings and smarts
Spirit is free to travel
but the body wants a home
People diverted my course
harnessed my power for the greed of their needs
altered the nature of things
destroyed homes, inundated
sacred places of repose
When oil slicks a cousin and when
pollution chokes a brother
I suffer since all flows together in the end
You are most of what I am

Show me what you are made of
Show me that you thirst for the waters of justice

Earth

From me came the Real People
who lived in balance with earth
Except some who became proud
and some who grew complacent

Awi Usdi spared hunters
who asked leave to kill the deer
giving thanks for sustenance
but if ritual was neglected

Little Deer would hunt them down
to inflict his punishment
of aching rheumatism
and still they failed to listen

Now ears are stoppered by buds
of technology, leaving
humans compromised for the sound
of the earth's lament

People hear what they want to
especially when powered by greed
like for gold: much grief ensued
But there are those who cherish

mountaintops, rivers, faces
of rocks, gauges of gorges
but vibrations from other
places tell of destruction—

how things got badly out of hand
out of balance, the right path lost
No wonder animals chose
to rise against you humans

but plants took pity on you
and took your part; even so
you continued to rebel
so Awi Usdi needed

a stronger and stealthier
messenger to command your
immediate attention
The Chief himself carried tick

and charged it with conveying
an unmistakable message
for when you're sick you will notice
another's condition; you see

that you are not separate
If you noticed trillium
you would see in its petals
past present future combined

But future is compromised
Inchworm tried to measure fault
and could not calculate it
Stay in the present: listen

or there will be no future
There are some chosen who take
on suffering for their people
through whose prayer of sacrifice

there is hope, through whose illness
the illness of the wider
world can hope to be redeemed
They pray Creator's will

be done within creation
not in some imagined place
The time is now, the battle is here
Who will follow Little Deer?

Where are all the warriors?
Who will fight for the given earth,
for animals and the water source?
Where are all my warriors?

Air

You ignore me until you start to fear
for your comfort then you complain, but only

when my illness impacts you like that dream
you had where: "there is no air"

As air, I despair of your coming clean
But I still give as freely as I can
even when clogged with smog of chemicals
I give so that you might live: *kenosis*
emptying of myself in your service
But it is hard to forgive all the slights
Which is why I am stirred when tobacco
is offered—prayers sent up with sacred smoke
This pleases and appeases me and makes
me feel there's hope of remedying hurt
You don't notice me until you can't breathe
then suddenly you can't get enough of me
This is what I call a fair-weather friend

Fire

When all was cold and dark
water spider carried spark
Even the small creatures do their part
(Now tick carries disease to jolt you from your ease
Disease can be purified by fire—
I burned contaminated blankets long ago
But cannot burn your blood although incensed
at all you've done and all you've failed to do)
        Not just anyone can start me, much less tend me
Only those who pay prayerful respect
Relationships take attention and intention

otherwise it is just parasitic
        Sometimes I flare in anger but generally
control my burn, especially for new growth
Burn victims agonize as necrotic skin
is debrided so new tissue can grow
It is hard to burn a tick; it resists longer than flesh
Awi Usdi needed an accomplice with tough armor
I can scatter and ruin all creatures and plants
even the insects hasten to escape
Yet tick will continue to feed as long as your blood flows
surviving onslaught
hidden on its host
attached to you
What are your attachments?
What feeds you?
I am most alive when those who honor
me dance around me, not worshipping me
as some have erroneously supposed
but through me worshipping the One who set
fire in the sky, fire in the hearth of their hearts
It is then I glow red with pleasure and cast sparks
skyward in celebration of tradition
Listen to story and song that elders
recount, sitting round my illumination
Once Little Deer stepped into my circle
of light, his white coat changed to glowing red
his antlers formed a delicate kindling
He tossed them as he stomped his little hooves
        Fire is your guardian, not your friend
No more turn your back to me than on the ocean—
one errant flame, one rogue wave can destroy you utterly

We elements keep faith with you if you
keep faith with us first; I yearn to help you
but you must learn your sacred medicine
Stop burning all your bridges

Awi Usdi

If at the critical moment
you remain silent instead
of saying what is needed
then you become complicit

You've lost your sense of balance
You've failed to ask permission
You've exceeded your allowance
so I have sent some justice

It hurts not to be Beloved
It hurts not to be honored
It hurts me that I hurt you
to garner your attention

Will you flee or fight?
Where are all my warriors?

Notes:

"Welcome Dance / War Dance": War/Welcome Dance: As danced by the Warriors of AniKituhwa, cultural ambassadors for the Eastern Band of Cherokee Indians, this dance was used historically not only when going to war, but also when meeting with other nations for diplomacy and peace while demonstrating strength. The dance was also used internally to raise money for those in need, with items placed on a blanket spread for that purpose. British Lt. Henry Timberlake described the dance in 1762: "the war dance gave me the greatest satisfaction, in that I had an opportunity of learning their methods of war."

"Creation": In the traditional Cherokee creation story, a turkey vulture or buzzard formed the mountains and valleys through movement of its wings.

"Copper": In biblical stories, Samson (Hebrew, Shimshon) was a legendary Israelite warrior and judge, who was renowned for the prodigious strength that he derived from his uncut hair.

"Target Practice": "Trickster" refers to the biblical story of Jacob, who, encouraged by his mother, Rebekah, fooled his blind and dying father Isaac into bestowing on him the blessing intended for his brother, Esau, thereby robbing his brother of his birthright. "Trickster" also alludes to the mythical trickster in Native American traditional stories that can take various forms, including coyote.

"Recruit": "Brek-ek-ek-ex, ko-ax, ko-ax" is the sound a chorus of frogs makes as Charon ferries Dionysus across a lake in Hades. Links to audio of *Pelophylax ridibundus,* a marsh frog common in Greece:

http://www.yalealumnimagazine.com/issues/2008_07/notebook.html
http://www.avisoft.com/sounds/frogs.wav

"In Tellico Plains": Tellico Plains was once the Cherokee town of Great Tellico, an important town of the Overhill Cherokee. Two significant trails met at Great Tellico: the Trading Path and the Warrior Path. Remnants of ceremonial/burial mounds were still visible in the 1960s.

"Code Talking": Cherokee was among the Native languages used by Code Talkers in both World Wars.

"Secret City": Oak Ridge, TN. Gregory Boertje-Obed, Sister Megan Rice, and Michael Walli were sentenced to time in federal prison for breaking in to the Y-12 National Security Complex, the "Fort Knox of Uranium," birthplace of the heart of the atomic bomb dropped on Hiroshima. Their act of "sabotage" was meant to draw public outrage over trillions spent on nuclear weapons since WWII. John Hendrix, an ascetic who lived in East Tennessee during the early 20th century, was nicknamed the Prophet of Oak Ridge after his death. He had heard a voice like a thunder clap telling him to sleep in the woods for 40 nights after which he had a vision of the future where, "Bear Creek valley some day will be filled with great buildings and factories and they will help toward winning the greatest war that ever will be.... They will be building things and there will be great noise and confusion and the earth will shake." His grave is located near Y-12. See the article "The Prophets of Oak Ridge," by Dan Zak, *The Washington Post.*

"Erasure": Underground warriors references the famous Terracotta Army, a collection of sculptures depicting the armies of Qin Shi Huang, the first Emperor of China. A form of funerary art, it was buried with the emperor in 210–209 BCE with the purpose of protecting him in the afterlife. The figures are life-sized and extremely detailed.

"Broken Formula to Bind One's Lover": in Cherokee culture there are many formulae for various intentions.

"Glass: A Fugue": In music, a fugue is a contrapuntal composition in which a short melody or phrase (the subject) is introduced by one part and successively taken up by others and developed by interweaving the parts. In psychiatry a fugue is a state or period of loss of awareness of one's identity, often coupled with flight from one's usual environment, associated with certain forms of conversion disorder (formerly misogynistically called "hysteria") and epilepsy

"Sacrifice": In Cherokee tradition, the bear used to be human. They are honored today in dance and song. Their claws adorn the necks of warriors and their fat is used in the making of warriors' paint.

"The Raven Mockers": In Cherokee tradition, malevolent forces that prey on the vulnerable dying. Strong prayers and medicine are needed to counteract their power.

"Nikwasi Warriors": Nikwasi Mound, Franklin, NC. Home to little soldiers (immortal spirit beings called Nunnehi) that spilled from the mound to defeat the Creek in a battle with the Cherokee. See Freeman Owle's account in *Living Stories of the Cherokee.* Originally topped by a townhouse, the mound held the sacred fire and was the dwelling place of the Nunnehi. In 1761 the British, former allies of the Cherokee, destroyed the houses and fields of Nikwasi and troops used the townhouse as a field hospital. In 1776 American troops again razed the town. In 1817 and 1819 North Carolina granted white settlers land to create the town of Franklin.

"Bound": Leading figure of the southeastern Cherokee, Nanye-hi, or Nancy Ward. Nanye-hi's husband was killed in a raid on the Creeks, the Cherokee's land rivals, during the 1755 Battle of Taliwa. Nanye-hi fought by his side, chewing the lead bullets for his rifle to make them more pointed and deadly. When the enemy killed him, she rallied the Cherokee warriors, leading a charge that brought victory to the Cherokees. Because of her actions, the Cherokee clans chose her as "Beloved Woman." As Beloved Woman, she headed the Women's Council, sat on the Council of Chiefs, and had complete power over prisoners.

"Morning Song": Facing East, a song of praise is offered in the morning. *Nogwo sunale nigalsda* (now morning has come). *Yona* (bear) *Gvyalielitse Yihowa* (I am thankful to you, God) *iyugwu* (colloquially, Bring it on).

“Questing”: Awi Usdi (Little Deer) punished hunters with crippling disease if they did not hunt responsibly, including offering prayer. The story of Awi Usdi teaches the need for balance. While this poem was written pre-pandemic, the interdependence of human and non-human animals has taken on even more urgency, given risk of viral transmissions. Written before George Floyd’s murder by police and his last words, “I can’t breathe.”

Acknowledgments

Thank you to the editors of the following journals where some of the poems first appeared, sometimes in different form:

The Pedestal Magazine: "Interrogation Room"

Poor Yorick: "The Late Unpleasantness"

Red Earth Review: "Yellow Tape" as "Black Hawks"

Bloodletters: "Survivor Song"

Toe Good: "Collateral Damage"

Rabbit and Rose: "Provisions"

Redheaded Stepchild: "Raven"

Silver Blade: "The Raven Mockers," "Morning Song"

Glint: "Copper"

Kalyna: "Creation"

Bared: Contemporary Art and Poetry on Bras and Breasts (La Femme Folles Books, 2017): "Bound"

Up the Staircase Quarterly: "Ceremony in lieu of a Funeral" (nominated for a Pushcart Prize)

With appreciation to
—Weymouth Center for the Arts & Humanities for a residency that afforded space and time to complete this manuscript
—Allison Adelle Hedge Coke for … everything and for asking what the tick was telling me: *gvgeyui ale atsvsdv*
—Gilliam Jackson for sending medicine when I needed it most
—Patients I was honored to know, in life and in death
—Marc Vincenz of MadHat Press for turning a box into a bird and other prestidigitations for conjuring the best out of this book

About the Author

Kimberly L. Becker is the author of three other poetry collections: *Words Facing East* and *The Dividings* (WordTech Editions), and *The Bed Book* (Spuyten Duyvil). Individual poems appear widely in journals and anthologies, including *Indigenous Message on Water; Women Write Resistance: Poets Resist Gender Violence;* and T*ending the Fire: Native Voices and Portraits.* She has held grants from Maryland, North Carolina, and New Jersey and residencies at Hambidge, Weymouth, and Wildacres. Reading venues include Busboys and Poets and The National Museum of the American Indian, Washington, DC. She has served as mentor for PEN America's Prison Writing and AWP's Writer to Writer programs. www.kimberlylbecker.com

Made in the USA
Las Vegas, NV
18 February 2021

18138072R00076